GALAXY OF SUPERSTARS

Leonardo DiCaprio

Hanson

LeAnn Rimes

Spice Girls

Jonathan Taylor Thomas

Venus Williams

CHELSEA HOUSE PUBLISHERS

GALAXY OF SUPERSTARS

Spice Girls

Nancy Shore

CHELSEA HOUSE PUBLISHERS
Philadelphia

Produced by
21st Century Publishing and Communications
a division of Tiger & Dragon International, Corp.
New York, New York
http://www.21cpc.com

Editor: Elaine Andrews
Picture Researcher: Hong Xiao
Electronic Composition and Production: Bill Kannar
Design and Art Direction: Irving S. Berman

CHELSEA HOUSE PUBLISHERS

Editor in Chief: Stephen Reginald
Managing Editor: James D. Gallagher
Production Manager: Pamela Loos
Art Director: Sara Davis
Director of Photography: Judy L. Hasday
Senior Production Editor: Lisa Chippendale
Publishing Coordinator: James McAvoy
Cover Illustration: Ian Varrassi

Front Cover Photo: AP/Wide World Photos
Back Cover Photo: AP/Wide World Photos

The Chelsea House World Wide Web site address is
http://www.chelseahouse.com

First Printing

1 3 5 7 9 8 6 4 2

Library of Congress Cataloging-in-Publication Data

Shore, Nancy.
   The Spice Girls / Nancy Shore.
      p.   cm.—(Galaxy of superstars)
   Includes bibliographical references and index.
   Summary: Presents the exploits of the popular British bubblegum
Group, the Spice Girls, covering their concerts, meetings with world
leaders and royalty, and personal histories.
   ISBN 0-7910-5149-8 (hc)
      1. Spice Girls—Juvenile literature. 2. Rock musicians—England—
Biography—Juvenile literature. 3. Women rock musicians—
England—Biography—Juvenile literature. [1. Spice Girls. 2. Musicians.
3. Women—Biography.] I. Title. II. Series.
ML3930.S715S56 1998
782.42166'092'2—dc21
[B]   98-42798
                                                          CIP
                                                       AC MN

CONTENTS

1

SPICE FEVER

It is November 1, 1997, and outside South Africa's Johannesburg Athletics Stadium, wildly excited teenage girls are screaming "HARRY! HARRY!" Used to constant public attention, the handsome, 13-year-old heir to the British throne is oblivious to the crowd. Surrounded by security guards, he heads backstage with his father, Prince Charles, to say a royal hello to five of his favorite British subjects—Posh, Sporty, Scary, Ginger, and Baby Spice. Prince Harry had just heard a foot-stomping, drums-pounding, back-flipping performance, at which the five pop idols rocked a stadium of adoring fans with their energetic, Girl-Powered brand of British bubble-gum pop. "If you wannabe my lover/You gotta get with my friends!"

The Spice Girls! The all-girl pop sensation whose debut album *Spice* had sold 19 million copies worldwide. The group whose adolescent antics, sexy chutzpah, and hip '90s' feminism—Girl Power—had become an irresistible wake-up call to young girls everywhere to take charge of their lives, wardrobes, and emotions. Riding the wave of dance-pop fever that made Take

---

Riding high on the wave of "spice fever" that has swept the pop-music world, the Spice Girls, each decked out in her own distinctive outfit, capture an audience with their bold, zany, and often boisterous brand of Girl Power.

That the most popular British boy group of the early '90s, the Spice Girls have infused their well-crafted hip-hop/reggae/rap/R&B/soul updates of '70s' funk with a fiercely independent, profemale stance. Their music was influenced by Madonna, riot-grrrl alternative rock, and the good-times credo of England's new "lad" culture.

Only this time it was not the lads who were having all the fun. It was the girls. For once they wanted to open the doors for the guys, help carry their school books, and then go out carousing with their girl buddies. "God help the mister, that comes between me and my sisters!" the Spice Girls declare in "Love Thing." They mean it! No British pop group since the Beatles had gained so much international attention.

Backstage, the normally reserved Prince Charles kissed each of the girls on the cheek. He had met the wildly popular group in May, after their performance at the Prince of Wales's Trust Concert in Manchester, England. (The trust is a charity to provide benefits to young people.) Geri Halliwell, the flamboyant leader of the pack, had broken royal decorum that night and, in a characteristic gesture of spicy Girl Power, had pinched the prince's royal behind. "We were all together for this photo shoot. . . . I thought I had to do something 'cos I might not get another chance, so I went for it!"

"Going for it" is a very big Spice Girl theme. When a Spice Girl wants something, from snaring a certain "hot" boy, to topping the *Billboard* charts with a smash-hit single,

to raising money for a war-torn African village, she does not waste time procrastinating. She pulls out all the stops and simply goes for it with every ounce of intelligence, wit, drive, and oomph she has. Eleven times out of 10 she gets it. Discussing the prince-pinching episode, Scary asked, "What did he feel like then?" Said Baby, "I bet he had strong, firm cheeks." Posh retorted, "He'll need them if he's going to be sitting on the throne all the time." Sporty responded, "Nah, I reckon he's all soft." This serious discussion of the royal posterior is typical of the spontaneous, fun-loving, down-to-earth Spices, who frequently dish out Spice-laden

Surrounding Prince Charles, the Girls (from left, Mel C, Geri, Emma, Mel B, and Victoria) laugh as Geri points to the lipstick marks on the prince's face. She had just planted a big kiss on the royal cheeks.

opinions about everything from British politics to comments about fellow performers.

In 1984, American pop star Cyndi Lauper sang the teenybopper hit "Girls Just Want to Have Fun!" The Spicy Ones have made that song their unspoken credo, along with Madonna's "Express Yourself." Madonna's self-conscious posing, high-powered dance tunes, and funky feminism have been major influences on the Girls. Feminism, yes, but fun feminism.

Emma, who read in the British press that at his exclusive boarding school, Prince Harry took down his poster of Pamela Anderson Lee and replaced it with one of her, gave the blushing young royal a warm hug. Arm in arm, the two princes and the five grinning girls, one in leopard spots, one with sporty exercise clothes, one wearing a chic designer dress, one in ribbon-tied pigtails, and one in a skintight dress, posed for 40 press photographers. Later that day the Girls met South Africa's President, Nelson Mandela, and his grandchildren. Calling the Girls his "heroes," President Mandela said, "It is one of the greatest moments of my life."

For the Spice Girls, who (except for Posh) come from working-class families, "hanging out" with Prince Charles, Prince Harry, and President Mandela must have seemed like a beautiful dream. After all, just a few years before, some of the Girls were living on "the dole" (British welfare), shopping in thrift shops, and eating beans and toast. Still, for the Fab Five, "chillin'" with the royals was

Emma and young Prince Harry meet at the Girls' concert in South Africa. With typical Spice Girl exuberance, Emma hugged the prince after learning she had replaced another female star to become his favorite.

the perfect expression of the Girl Power that had propelled them to the top of the pop charts. If you stand up for your beliefs, don't let others boss you around, surround yourself with supportive friends, work hard, and pursue your dreams, anything and everything is possible!

The unstoppable quintet were determined to dress the way they wanted and to lay down the law about friendship, love, and sex. After signing with Virgin Records, their hit single "Wannabe" was released in July 1996. It skyrocketed to number one in Britain and in 31 other countries. *Spice*, released in November, quickly became the biggest-selling British album of 1996. In January 1997, "Wannabe" hit U.S. *Billboard*

Prince Charles introduces the Girls to President Nelson Mandela, who greets them at his residence. In welcoming the Girls, whose concert in Johannesburg was a charity benefit, Mandela told them they were his "heroes."

charts at number 11—the highest entry for any British band in the United Sates—before zooming to number one. *Spice World*, the movie, was one of the biggest box-office smashes of 1998; *Spice World*, the album, was another international chart topper.

Each Spice Girl has a distinctly different personality. Scary Mel B is loud and proud, always "on," ready for a good time, and proud of her mixed-race heritage. Posh Victoria is reserved and discriminating, with a cool sophistication and a dry, tongue-in-cheek humor. Sporty Mel C, a superorganized early riser, projects a girl-next-door normality. Cute, giggly, and girlish, Baby

Emma is also warm, tender, and loving. But watch out, Emma has a blue belt in karate. Ginger, or Sexy Geri, is a zany temptress with flashes of wit and intelligence, always ready to defend Girl Power. As different as they are, all five have one thing in common: they knew at an early age that they wanted to be performers, and each had her own special talents and dreams, with a touch of star quality.

"I wanna really, really, really wanna zigazig ha!" In the past two years the world's young people have had their hearts, minds, and eardrums seasoned with a very unusual brand of spice. Girls, and boys, have been ignited by the naughty but nice, serious but fun-loving, sane but crazy, all dressed up and a zillion places to go vixens of Girl Power—the Spice Girls. This is how it all began.

2

THE EARLY YEARS

Geraldine Estelle Halliwell was born August 6, 1972. She was educated in Spain, her mother's homeland, before her family moved to Watford, a London suburb. Her mother works as a cleaner, and her father, who died in 1994, was a car dealer. The youngest of two older brothers and two older sisters, Geri was drawn to music, dance, and playacting at an early age and delighted in performing. With sister Natalie strumming an imaginary guitar, and using a hairbrush as a microphone, Geri often put on pop concerts for family and friends. "She always had a deep, strong, husky voice. No one could believe that kind of voice came out of such a little person," recalls Natalie. The voice of this "little person" was heard in public when she made her first appearance in a school play as an alien with one line: "Has earth got a dark half, like us?"

When Geri was 11, her mother enrolled her in the straitlaced Watford Girls School. (As a member of Jehovah's Witnesses, Geri's mother disapproved of worldly behavior, including celebrating holidays.) With her outgoing personality, frequent dress-code violations

---

It is as much their uninhibited, in-your-face style as their music that has rocketed the Spice Girls to the top of the pop charts. They have traveled a long way in a short time from their early beginnings, when their dreams of becoming stars were only just dreams.

Geri, "Ginger Spice," signs autographs for fans. Known as the most talkative of the group, Geri is the loudest when it comes to shouting "Girl Power."

(short skirts and eyeliner), and willingness to debate her classmates on such controversial subjects as striking to protest poor working conditions, Geri became known as an outspoken rebel. She also became enamored of pop music stars. At age 12, she idolized George Michael, Elvis Presley, and her early role model, Madonna.

When she was 16, Geri left home for a rented room in Watford. On her own, she studied tourism and travel as well as English literature, one of her favorite subjects. Geri was eager to see the world, however. Now a five-foot-two, blue-eyed, red-haired beauty, she got a job dancing at London's Astoria Club. The chance to travel came in 1991 when she was offered a dancing job at one of Europe's biggest clubs, the BCM in Majorca, Spain. From there, in search of further adventure, Geri went on to Turkey, where she was hired to display prizes on a TV game show.

Back again in England, the unstoppable Geri worked as an aerobics instructor, barmaid, and cleaner while auditioning for shows and TV extra spots. Geri also posed nude for *Page Three*, a popular section of British newspapers. The pictures resurfaced in the media once the Spice Girls became a household name. By then, Geri was having too much fun to notice. "I'd like to be remembered as a wild freedom-fighter with method in her madness," Geri wrote in the group's book *Spice Girls: Girl Power!*

Melanie Jayne Chisholm was born January 12, 1974, in Liverpool, a northern industrial city. Her mother sang in bands and her father was an elevator repairman. When Mel was eight, her parents divorced. She, her mother, and her brother, Jad, moved to Widnes, a small Liverpool suburb, where her mother worked as a secretary. "She brought me up on a lot of Motown, The Beatles, Deep Purple, Rainbow," Mel told *Melody Maker.* Mel's mother remarried a rock musician-cabdriver, and the family lived in a rough, working–class neighborhood. However, Mel was a cheerful girl, who was thankful for what she had and determined to make the most of herself. In her first stage appearance at three, she sang "Beside the Seaside" with lots of knee bends and toe points.

Reflecting her Spice name, "Sporty," Mel C favors athletic outfits. She prefers to proclaim Girl Power with a tattoo symbolizing women and strength.

In junior high school, Mel loved practicing handstands and playing football (English soccer). Music was also one of her passions. *Top of the Pops*, a weekly pop–music show was a favorite, and when she bought her first album, *The Kids from Fame*, she would perform the whole show in her living room. Mel often dressed up like a showgirl and practiced singing. At 14, she got a corkscrew perm, wore baggy jeans, Reeboks, and a dollar-sign necklace like her idol, British pop singer Neneh Cherry, who was an early influence. She was also a big fan of George Michael, Stevie Wonder, Madonna, and the popular British boy band Bros.

At Fairfield County High School, future pop star "Sporty" played hockey, center on the netball team, was an accomplished gymnast who won lots of prizes, and excelled at French. She also acted in school productions of *Annie*, *The Wiz*, and *Blood Brothers* and sang in the school choir.

As a teenager, Mel had a difficult time coping with her parents' divorce. Her mother had another son, Paul, and her father also remarried. Mel felt as if she did not fit in anywhere. (Today she feels lucky to have two close, supportive, and loving families.) After spending three years at the Doreen Bird Performing Arts College in Kent, Mel moved to London, working as a backup singer and auditioning for West End shows.

"A bloke's best chatup line with me would be an invitation to a football match. I'm really not interested in restaurants, romance, and all that," Mel wrote in *Spice Girls: Girl Power!* An enthusiastic football fan, Mel also plays whenever she can for the Rickmansworth Ladies Soccer Club in Hertfordshire. At five-foot-six with hazel eyes, a nose ring, and tattoos on her right arm and shoulder symbolizing women and strength, charismatic Mel C is a hardworking perfectionist. "With everything, I think that if you're going to do something, you should do it well," she wrote in the book *Real Life: Real Spice.*

Victoria Addams was born on April 7, 1974. Her father was in a '60s' rock band, but when he started his own electrical-equipment company, he became wealthy. Victoria grew up in a large, wood-beamed house in Goffs' Oak, Hertfordshire, with her sister, Louise, and brother, Christian. Although the Addamses took yearly vacations in Europe, the children were not spoiled. If Victoria wanted something, she had to wait for a special occasion. Her parents always stressed the importance of sharing with others.

Like Geri and Mel, Victoria loved music from an early age. Along with her favorite TV show, *Top of the Pops*, she idolized Matt Goss of Bros and ballet star Rudolph Nuryev. Early on she expressed her joy in singing and acting when she appeared in her earliest performances—*The Pied Piper* and *Frosty the Snowman*. When, at eight years old, Victoria enrolled at the Jason Theatre School, her teacher, Joy Spriggs, recalled: "Victoria ate, slept, and drank dancing."

For Victoria, the adulation that has come with success is a new experience. She was not popular in high school. A quiet, well-behaved, serious student, Victoria's classmates saw her as a goody-goody, and she was ostracized. "I never had loads of friends . . . but I had to grin and bear it. . . . It taught me that being the most popular girl in school isn't the most important thing in the world," she later wrote. Nevertheless, she thoroughly enjoyed art and dance classes.

After graduation at 16, Victoria attended a three-year course at Laine Theatre Arts School in Epsom, Surrey, and she shared an apartment with four other dancers. (Her sister, Louise, remembers tights always hanging in the bathroom but no food in the place.) Victoria was finally in her element. Instructor Betty Laine has said: "She trained in dance, singing, and acting, but . . . if they're going into the pop field, image is very important. And she took this extremely seriously. . . ."

At five-foot-six, Victoria was tall enough to be a professional dancer. For a time, she toured with a theater company and became

"Posh Spice" Victoria, who has been described as the "cool" Spice, says she does not really like her smile and claims she is not so posh. But she can be caught smiling, and she does love designer outfits.

another young hopeful making the rounds on the audition circuit. Although "Posh" Victoria is famous today for her love of designer clothes, there is a lot more to this intelligent, talented, and very funny young woman than labels like Prada and Gucci. "I'm far from posh. I don't talk posh and I don't think of myself as posh," she wrote in *Spice Girls: Girl Power!*

Melanie Janine Brown was born on May 29, 1975, in Leeds, an industrial town in northern England. She is the child of an interracial marriage. Her father, an engineer, is from the Caribbean island of Nevis. Mel's mother works in a department store. In the 1970s in Britain, interracial couples still faced prejudice. Mel recalls sitting on her father's lap on the bus because her mother thought no one would bother a black man holding a baby of color. As a mixed-race child, Mel was teased by other children. Today, tolerance is a major part of Mel's Girl Power credo. She believes that whatever color you are, wherever you come from, whether you are overweight or skinny, however you like to dress, you should make your opinion heard.

As a child, Mel loved making up dances, recording her own radio programs, and putting on shows. When she was six, she made her first stage appearance as a clown in a school play. Because she could not afford to go to pop concerts, the first one she saw was Janet Jackson with the Spice Girls.

In her early teens, fun-loving Mel dressed like pop star Neneh Cherry and hung out with a neighborhood girl gang. Often in trouble for being the wildest student at school, Mel once persuaded a boyfriend to dress up in her mother's clothes—with high heels and a necklace. "We watched all the cars stopping as he walked over to the shop. . . . We never spoke to our neighbors because they thought we were completely mad!"

Mel had a more serious side as well. She took acting and ballet lessons and was accepted at the Intake School of Performing Arts in Leeds. Later, Mel was accepted at the prestigious Northern School of Contemporary Dance in Leeds, but she was more advanced than the other students and did not stay long. After dislocating her knee in a school show, Mel was told she would never dance again. Her spirit was so strong, however, that she quickly recovered.

In high school, Mel worked hard in dance, music, and drama and excelled in English. Mel's father was very strict about education, and if her grades did not improve each year, he would cut her dance classes. So she had to study hard.

At 17 Mel won the Miss *Leeds Weekly News* beauty contest, receiving a Renault Clio award for a year and a trip to Disneyland. After graduation, Mel studied voice and percussion, taught aerobics, sold newspaper ads, and took a job dancing in a men's club.

Now a five-foot-five, brown-eyed dynamo with "big hair," who could dance up a storm, Mel auditioned for several musicals in London, appeared in a shoe commercial, did walk-on parts, and took dance and voice

Receiving an award as the Female Spectacle Wearer of the Year, Mel B flashes the victory sign. With her crown of curly hair, pierced tongue, and signature leopard outfits, "Scary Spice" is a dynamo onstage and off.

Emma, "Baby Spice," does not usually appear in a floor-length gown with a fur wrap. She once claimed she did not want to be a "cutie," but her trademark attire is pigtails and baby-doll outfits.

lessons. In one of her theater appearances, she was fired for giggling too much onstage, and her agent said she would never work again. He certainly could not have been more wrong.

With her "Scary" leopard outfits, pierced tongue, and a Japanese "spirit, heart, and mind" tattoo on her stomach, the strong-willed Mel B injects a huge boost of kinetic energy into the Spice Girls. As Mel has said, she is happiest when she is onstage perform-ing. "Letting rip onstage, doing your thing and just going for it. I love that!"

Emma Lee Bunton was born on January 21, 1976, in Finchley, North London. An adorable blonde, blue-eyed child with a bright, happy smile, Emma was entered in a beauty contest at three years old—and won. She also began ballet, jazz, and tap classes at that ten-der age and made her first stage appearance as a swan. Emma soon signed with a modeling agency and began appearing regularly in chil-dren's clothing catalogs. Her face became familiar to British viewers when she was cast in TV commercials. Coincidentally, when she was eight, she appeared in a musical show with Victoria.

Emma's parents divorced when she was 11. Fortunately, however, the breakup did not create havoc in her young life. Her teenage years were happy and exciting as she enjoyed musical films, attended live concerts, and wrote songs. Emma invented her own radio stations and pretended to be the disc jockeys. She often held parties at which all the girls had to dress like Madonna.

With money from her modeling, Emma studied dance, drama, and singing at a stage school in London. Surrounded by talented teens, she was in her element. At 14, Emma was offered a scholarship at the school. It was a lucky break, since her parents could no longer afford the tuition. Emma enjoyed another lucky break by studying voice with the vocal coach who would later ask her to audition for the "all-girl band" that would become the Spice Girls.

Underneath her calm, cheerful, "little-girl" exterior lurks a straightforward, no-nonsense young woman. Emma wears her hair in pigtails, loves lollipops, cotton candy, and all things fluffy and cuddly. But this five-foot-two "baby doll" has a blue belt in karate, a martial art she learned from her black-belt mom. Emma can smile her way out of any jam. She can also floor someone if necessary. As she wrote in *Spice Girls: Girl Power!* "The appeal of the Spice Girls is our honesty. We're not perfect and people like us for that."

3

WANNABES

In November 1996, the Spice Girls turned on London's Christmas Lights in Oxford Street before a cheering crowd of thousands who were probably not aware that the quintet's story had started just a few blocks away, at the Danceworks Studio. Two years earlier, when the five unknowns were on the London audition circuit, Bob Herbert, his son Chris, and Chic Murphy, an experienced London manager, came up with the idea of creating a girl group. They placed an ad in London's *Stage* for "an all female act for a record deal." It read: "R.U. 18-23 with the ability to sing/dance? R.U. streetwise, outgoing, ambitious and dedicated?"

More than 400 hopefuls showed up. After some weeding out, about 100 girls, including Victoria and the two Mels, remained to perform jazz-dance routines, harmonize on songs, and sing solo to piano accompaniment. The Herberts were not only looking for singing and dancing ability. They wanted five girls with that special charisma that would make music-industry executives take notice. Victoria, the two Mels, and a girl named Michelle Stephenson made the final list of 10 for the second

---

For the Spice Girls, being friends and having fun together is as important as their music. Their first hit song, "Wannabe," expressed this credo when it proclaimed friendship was better than a love affair.

audition. Geri, who had missed the first audition, phoned Chris Herbert and, with her go-get-'em personality, convinced him to let her audition.

In April 1994, the five began working on songs and dance routines at Ian Lee's Trinity Studio outside London. The Herberts wanted to see if the young women would work well together. Deciding that they did, the Herberts asked each whether she wanted to make a long-term commitment. Singing and dance training would be intense, and fame and success were a possibility. The Herberts could not promise anything. All that was certain was that months and months of hard work lay ahead. All five were gung ho.

So that the five could live, work, and train together, and really get to know each other, the Herberts rented a house, paid the bills, and gave each a small stipend. The five began training daily at Trinity Studio with vocal coach Pepi Lemer. "They were shaking and when they sang their voices were wobbling. . . . My first impression was 'My God, there's a lot of work to be done here,'" Lemer told the *Daily Mail.* Lemer guided them through grueling vocal sessions, repeating notes, phrases, and harmonies again and again. Through headaches and outbursts of frayed nerves, Lemer pushed the five to keep going. It was obvious from the start there was something special here.

In July 1994, Michelle Stephenson was accepted at a drama school, and she opted out. The Herberts needed someone with the right chemistry to blend in with the others. Lemer recalled an attractive, talented girl who had once been her vocal pupil, a perky blonde named Emma Bunton. When Lemer tracked down Emma, she jumped at the opportunity. After a quick audition, Emma was in. "I was the missing piece of the jigsaw puzzle," Emma told America Online.

The five's day began with an hour of dance and vocal warm-up exercises and proceeded to dance routines, vocal harmonies, brainstorming, and trying out different ideas. Vocal sessions with Lemer intensified, and a distinctive sound began to emerge. "The Spice Girls already had the ambition and wanted success and fame. I didn't teach them that. . . . They just wanted to know how to get there," said Lemer.

Sessions were not always smooth. Sometimes arguments erupted over a particular dance routine, or who should sing what, or whether someone was singing the right note. The five never lost sight of their goal, however. Sometimes they worked until 7 or 8 P.M., going over the same routines until they got them absolutely perfect. Often they went home at night and came back in the morning with a new song or routine. "We'd all make dinner and chill out for the evening," wrote Emma. "But for us relaxing was sitting down and writing a song. . . ."

By fall 1994, their singing style had come a long way from the shaky, off-key voices Lemer had heard at the auditions. Something powerful was emerging. But the group still did not have a name. They found it when songwriter Tim Hawes collaborated with the five on "Sugar and Spice," and Geri suddenly was struck with the name—"Spice" was ideal! The rest of them loved it. And so the Spice Girls were born.

Despite grueling training sessions, the Girls could sometimes relax. Together they practiced vocals and dance, harmonized, brainstormed ideas, and wrote songs, developing the music and style that would make them world famous.

Among the five, Geri lacked formal singing and dance training, and she wanted to rehearse and rehearse. This lead to some loud confrontations with strong-willed Mel B, while diplomatic Mel C played the peacemaker. Eventually differences were ironed out, and a real sisterhood developed. Hard work and tight living quarters broke down inhibitions, and the Girls grew to accept one another's strengths and weaknesses. "It was like Girls Behaving Badly," Victoria says in the 1997 video *Girl Power! Live in Istanbul.* "But it was a really good foundation for us because we got to learn about each other. And now, I think, we're closer than friends. We're totally honest and upfront with each other."

Determination and hard work were paying off. "By December of ninety-four, you had a really professional, tight band that shouted success. And that didn't come easy. They had to work really hard," said Ian Lee. "In the early days we knew there was star quality. . . . You never imagined it would be quite so big. But we knew they were going to make it."

At the end of 1994, the Herberts staged a showcase for the quintet. Exploding with raw energy, the Spice Girls sang five songs and performed their funky, high-powered dance routines. The showcase generated a huge buzz in the British pop-music world. Here were five sexy, smart, sassy girls who overflowed with personality. Individually they were not great singers, but together they were phenomenal. With the right record label they could be the next big thing. Agents bombarded the Herberts with offers, and soon record companies began requesting tapes.

Encouraged by the overwhelmingly positive response to the showcase, the Girls began working even harder. Trouble was brewing in paradise, however. The gulf between the Herberts' ideas and the Spice Girls' ideas of who the Spice Girls were began to widen. During the long months of work, the five had bonded, developed a stronger, clearer sense of themselves, and had begun to see the world with new eyes.

According to the Girls, the Herberts wanted a combo with one lead and four backup singers. They wanted to be five equal members, sharing the spotlight individually at times and together at others. The Girls began making up melodies and writing their own lyrics, and Geri and Mel B came up with the idea of writing raps. "I hate the way some people try and conform, just because they're scared that they're going to make a bad impression. I say: 'just do it!'" Mel B wrote. Loud, and sometimes lewd, the Girls wrote songs about relationships as they would like them to be—equal and honest. They began telling the guys to get real or get lost.

In a July 1997 *Rolling Stone* interview, Bob Herbert insisted the Girls were never told to dress alike and that the whole point of the auditions was to find five strikingly different young women. But the Herberts had created a Frankenstein monster that now wanted to go off on its own. The Girls decided not to sign a management contract with the Herberts. Packing up their belongings, the Girls drove around the countryside in Geri's car with their catalog of songs and dance routines, determined to find a new manager. "We had so many managers saying 'Dress like this, sing that song, I can make you big stars,'" Mel B told *Music Week*.

The Girls got a break when Simon Fuller, a young successful manager, heard one of their songs. In March 1995, the Girls signed a contract with Fuller, who introduced them to talented young songwriters. "Wannabe" was one of their first collaborations with Richard Stannard and Matt Rowe.

"We worked with soul boys and remixers who were undiscovered and open to letting us lean over their shoulder and say, 'Would you turn up that bass line,'" Geri told *DJ Times*. In *Rolling Stone*, Mel C described the Girls' songwriting process. "I'm better at melodies, but I'm terrible with lyrics. Geri's brilliant with lyrics. Emma's great with harmonies. Mel B always comes up with hooks. And Victoria's great with melody as well. We never get stuck."

In spring 1995, the Girls chose 14 from their impressive catalog of 35 songs for a debut album. Still not signed to a label, they began making impromptu appearances at industry parties and roller-blading uninvited into the offices of record executives, singing their songs a cappella. "I'll never forget the day they burst in here," Virgin Records executive Ashley Newton told *Music Week*. "They caused such a commotion, doing a mad routine in the office, all talking at once and being really funny." When Newton heard "Something Kinda' Funny," he was hooked.

Inundated with offers, the Girls chose Virgin, where they would have the freedom to be themselves. With a hefty advance from Virgin, suddenly the Spice Girls could afford to dine on more than beans and toast. One of the first things the group did after signing with Virgin was throw a party for their parents. Their families had supported the Girls in all their difficulties, and now it was time to share their success. An influential manager now supported their vision, talented musical producers translated their songwriting efforts, a major record company was behind them, and they had money in the bank. The Girls could stop worrying about basic necessities and start doing what they loved most—writing songs, creating dance routines, and performing. The Spice invasion had begun.

4

WE'RE NUMBER ONE!

Virgin was determined that its hot new band would burst on the music scene with a bang. The Girls were eager not to disappoint their managers. In October 1995, when they were introduced to the press at England's exclusive Kempton Races, the Spices jumped on top of the statue of the famous racehorse Red Rum, got shouted at by racetrack security, and sang "Wannabe" a cappella. In November, the Girls flew to Los Angeles, California, for a promotional tour, where they received star treatment.

Back in London, the five hunkered down for a period of hard work—creating melodies and harmonies for the *Spice* album. Lyrics were revised again and again, while musical teams including Absolute, Biff 'n Memphis, and Kennedy and Baylis backed them up. With the experience gained during months of practicing harmonies and freestyling off each other, the five Spices finally recorded the all-important vocals. Stationed in separate, glass-encased booths, each listened to tracks through headphones. Long days became long nights as the Girls recorded take after take of the same line or verse until it was absolutely perfect. On the morning they were to

---

The Girls' concert tours brought them international fame and made them number one in the hearts of their fans, scores of whom gathered outside a hotel in Rome to cheer an impromptu Spice Girls performance from a balcony.

record "Love Thing," Geri arrived late. Blushing with excitement, she announced a special anniversary and gave each girl a gold ring inscribed "Spice." The Spice Girls now had their special good-luck charms.

By December 1995, *Spice* was completed under the watchful eyes and ears of the Girls. Now the five began working on choreography for their upcoming videos and performances. Shopping for new clothes was next. Each girl took her individual style to the max. For Mel B it is a cross between Lenny Kravitz and Prince and outrageously tight. Mel C took a step up from her signature trakkies, deciding on smart hipster trousers and little tank tops. Emma likes a funky look—short skirts and tight shirts—but fancies up her outfits with frilly socks. Geri mixes glamorous clothes with retro thrift-shop outfits. For Victoria, it is designer fashions.

In April 1996, the first of what was soon to become a weekly deluge of press articles about the Girls appeared in *Music Week*, proclaiming, "The boys with guitars had better prepare for battle." The "boys" would have to battle "Wannabe," the Girls' debut single. "We were just having a laugh in the studio when we wrote 'Wannabe,'" Mel B wrote in *Real Life: Real Spice.* "It had no sit-down planning. The sentiment, the meaning, the lyrics, the rhythm just happened." Aware that a debut single usually gets very little attention, the Girls wanted to save their better material for later. Little did they, or Virgin, know what was in store.

"Wannabe" was accompanied by a video in which the Girls create havoc at a swank London

Emma and Geri set out on a shopping expedition. Each of the five carefully chooses her outfit to express her individualism and the image she wants to project.

club, running around and dancing on table-tops. The wild climax is punctuated by Mel C's athletic backflips. "It wasn't very controlled. . . . We wanted the camera to capture the madness of the Spice Girls," wrote Geri. When a British cable show aired a sneak preview of "Wannabe," switchboards were jammed. "Who were they?" "What was the release date?" The Girls followed up with a specially filmed video clip introducing viewers to the Spices.

Buoyed by the unexpected buzz, the Girls went on a promotional tour, singing live on radio stations and at seaside resorts, clowning around, spouting Girl Power, and generally shaking up the English countryside.

Riding a wave of growing excitement, the Girls flew to Los Angeles to learn kung fu for their next video. They made headlines when Emma, Geri, and Mel B dashed stark naked down the corridor of the Four Seasons Hotel. "I feel alive when I do mad things," declared Mel B.

Back in London, "Wannabe" was released. It shot to number three on the charts the first week and began selling out of record stores immediately. The Girls were invited to appear on *Top of the Pops*, the show they all had watched since childhood. The show's popular teen magazine had published their special nicknames: Ginger, Sporty, Posh, Baby, and Scary, along with an illustration of a spice rack.

Onstage, instead of seasoned professionals, the five came across as the girls next door just having a lot of fun and laughs, and Britain fell in love with them immediately. Young girls embraced these cheeky new role models—and boys did not know what hit them. "Wannabe" shot straight to number one on July 27, making the Spice Girls the first British group ever to top the charts with a debut single. "Who's your favorite Spice Girl?" was the question on everyone's lips. Magazines and newspapers began falling over themselves to print stories and interviews. *Q Magazine* wrote: "In the way that Neneh Cherry's 'Buffalo Stance' touched the right girlpower buttons with its mix of rap, soul and attitude, so . . . 'Wannabe' combines reggae with feisty pop."

Sales records began to fall like ninepins. "Wannabe" stayed at number one in Britain for a whopping seven weeks. In its fourth week, it went platinum. By the time it dropped to number three it had sold 1.25 million copies in Britain alone. Virgin executives were thrilled. The company began flying the Girls around Europe, and everywhere they went they appeared on the covers of popular magazines. "They're sexy, they're fresh, they're revolutionary, and their music is really cool," proclaimed *Bravo*, Germany's leading teen magazine. An in-store signing in Madrid, Spain, drew 10,000 fans. "What does 'zigazig ha' mean?" everyone asked. The Girls were evasive. The memorable line has different meanings for different people.

In September the Girls flew to California's Mojave Desert to film the flashy '60s'-style "Say You'll Be There" video. Wearing futuristic costumes, they performed kung-fu kicks and punches in an extravagant display of Girl Power. "This was one of my favorite videos," Emma wrote. "We were out in the desert and we were all getting along really well, so it was a complete laugh."

The single "Say You'll Be There" was released in October. The funky, romantic R&B jam that gave each girl a chance to show off her own voice and personality went straight to number one. It sold 350,000 copies its first week and went platinum the second. "The song has got to do with what we've been through together. We've always been there for each other," said Mel C.

Expressing their delight, the Girls accept one of their many awards, this one from MTV for Best Dance Video for their song "Wannabe."

The Spice Girls could not have imagined that success and fame would come so fast. "The support has been unbelievable," Victoria summed it up. "We're living our wildest dreams!" Suddenly the Spice Girls were every-where—on the radio, in magazines, on TV, even drawing the national lottery numbers. On November 4, 1996, *Spice* was released in Britain. The album immediately shot to number one and sold two million copies in two weeks. Reviews were wildly enthusiastic. The influential *New Musical Express* deemed *Spice* "a pop soul classic." By the time the Girls ceremoniously switched on London's Christmas Lights, "Wannabe" had hit number one in 31 countries—injecting new life into the British pop-music industry.

The press could not get enough. On a pre-Christmas trip to Lapland, the snow-suited Spices were dogged by 200 journalists and cameramen. When Geri dubbed former Prime Minister Margaret Thatcher "the first Spice Girl, the pioneer of our ideology Girl Power" in the conservative *Spectator*, the tabloids went wild, linking the group with the Conservatives and speculating on whether the "Spice Vote" would be a factor in the upcoming election. Emma and Victoria did not mind, but Liverpool-raised Mel C was staunchly pro-Labour, and Mel B declared herself an anarchist. "I wasn't claiming I was a real Tory [a Conservative]. I just admire people with ideals. . . . I respect the fact that it takes dedication and guts to stand up and say what you believe in," Geri explained.

"2Become1," a sultry love ballad with a safe-sex message was released on December 16. An appealing video set against the romantic New York City skyline helped the single skyrocket to number one. By December 22, it had sold more than 500,000 copies, making it the fastest-selling record of the year. In a reader's poll in *Smash Hits*, a British pop magazine, the Spice Girls were awarded Best British Act, Best New Act, and Best Video. At the awards ceremony at the London Arena, they sang "Wannabe" and "Say You'll Be There" to a wildly enthusiastic

Screaming and reaching out for the Girls, fans in Switzerland nearly topple a fence to get to their idols.

audience. Hosting the *Top of the Pops* Christmas Day special, they clowned, wore Marx Brothers' disguises, poked fun at each other, and told the guys what was what before performing their songs. When the BRIT Awards (the English Grammies) nominations were announced, the Girls were in the running for Best Video, Best British Single, Best Newcomer, and Best British Group.

Spice had been the biggest-selling album of 1996. The songs had proved a perfect confection of modern pop genius. Fusing a wide range of musical styles with easy-to-remember lyrics, a driving danceable beat, and a unique, empowering message that love involves give and take and that true friendships are more important than superficial romances, the album made young girls feel strong, attractive, and in control.

In a few short months, the Spice Girls had skyrocketed to international stardom. Bodyguards protected them from tabloid photographers and hordes of screaming fans, and secretaries answered fan mail. Their lives had become a nonstop round of plane trips, interviews, performances, and public appearances. "We get schedules every day—on them is what we're doing every minute, sometimes from 6 A.M. to midnight. You can't look at more than one at a time or you'd go mad," Mel B wrote in *Spice Girls: Girl Power!*

Before their all important U.S. debut, the Girls took a short, much-needed vacation. Emma and her mother went to Barbados, and Mel B visited her father's family in the Caribbean. Mel C jetted to the Middle East with her mother and stepfather, while Geri relaxed in private somewhere with a lot of sun and sand. In their different corners of the globe, all five knew that these few precious weeks of rest only represented the calm before the storm. The United States, still uncharted territory, was their next target. The Spice rack was full to the brim. And in 1997, Spicemania would explode.

5

SPICEMANIA

Virgin had purposely waited until the Spice Girls had a huge fan base in Britain and the rest of the globe before releasing their records in the United States, the world's biggest music market. Determined to take the country by storm, in January 1997, the Girls flew to New York City to kick off a promotional tour. "Wannabe" had sold a whopping eight million copies, and *Spice*, five million, worldwide. "We knew we had to start from the beginning and earn respect, and that's what we did," wrote Victoria. They gave their first U.S. concert at the Hialeah racetrack in Miami, Florida, for a crowd of 2,000 before moving across the heartland to Los Angeles.

Between appearances they visited local radio stations to meet programmers and DJs. "Wannabe," released on January 24, smashed into U.S. *Billboard* charts at number 11, the highest entry ever for a British band. When *Spice* was released on February 4, "Wannabe" had climbed to number four. "Outside radio stations and hotels they keep singing 'Wannabe' to us," Mel C said, "but in American accents!"

"Spicemania" was in full swing when Victoria and Geri appeared at the BRIT awards ceremony in London. Victoria bared her midriff, while Geri was wrapped in a miniskirt British flag with a peace symbol on the back.

"Wannabe" soon hit number one and *Spice* was lodged firmly in the Top 10. *Teen* magazine ran a fashion spread, proclaiming the five new heroines for girls. *Entertainment Weekly* wrote: "There's something endearing about this goofily formulaic Euro Pop." *Time* magazine declared that their message was "Hello, we're sexy British gals! Let's make music fun again!" and *Newsweek* branded them simply "adorable." As Mel B told MTV's Kurt Loder, however, "We're so close . . . we don't really care what anybody says! As long as we're having fun, that's the whole vibe of it all. . . . And hopefully we're giving out positive messages. . . ." In an interview with a Seattle radio station, when the male DJ jokingly suggested that the Girls drop the English "fellows" and pick up some American "guys," the five went wild. "This is about Girl Power," insisted Mel B. "This is not about picking up guys. . . . It's about creating a positive vibe. . . ." She declared, "We don't need men to control our lives."

Back in Britain, the first issue of *Spice*, the official Spice Girl magazine, hit the stands in late January, featuring a "Spice Advice" section from which fans could get candid answers on everything from boyfriends to homework. After the Internet had exploded with hundreds of Spice Girl websites, Virgin launched an official site featuring interviews, song lyrics, video clips, Spice Girls facts, merchandise, and fans' comments and stories. "Tips & Hints" featured such helpful advice from the Girls as Mel B's "Be as outrageous and as mad as you possibly can, even if you're by yourself!" and Victoria's "If you haven't got it, fake it."

In mid-February the Girls flew back to Britain, where they filmed the video "Mama" before a jam-packed audience of kids and parents. Meant as a thank–you, the Spices sang to their real mothers in the audience. "I was looking up at my mum and crying, because it was about us. . . . I think it will always affect me in that way, especially when I'm abroad," Emma wrote. With royalties from *Spice* flowing in, the Girls shared their new-found wealth with their families. "My mum's done so much for me," wrote Mel C, "I want her to share in what I've got."

After performing at Cash for Kids, a charity concert in Birmingham, the Girls jetted to Dublin, Ireland, for the Irish Music Awards, which had voted them the Best International Act. They then had three days to prepare for the all-important BRIT Awards on February 24, which would be shown on national TV to more than nine million viewers. Nominated in five categories, the five had been invited to open the show.

When they burst onstage at London's Earls' Court Arena with a medley of "Wannabe" and "Who Do You Think You Are," the crowd went wild, rising to its feet. "We couldn't believe we were opening the show. When we were facing the back of the stage, we were all screaming!" Mel C wrote. Geri felt "proud that we were doing a dance we made up in a tiny little beaten up recording studio in front of all those people and cameras." Geri's outfit, a minidress with the British flag

The Spice Girls give generously of their time for charity concerts. Here they launch the 1997 Poppy Appeal, a benefit fund to aid families of Britain's war dead.

on the front and a peace symbol on the back, stole the show. The hit of the evening, the Spices won Best Single ("Wannabe") and Best Video (*Say You'll Be There*). The following day, British newspapers hailed the Spice Girls' triumph.

In March, "Mama/Who Do You Think You Are" was released in Britain, becoming the

Girls' fourth number one hit. "Mama" struck a national chord in homes all over the country, especially on Britain's Mother's Day, March 9. On March 14, the Girls appeared with the look-alike group, Sugar Lumps, at a benefit for the homeless called Red Nose Day. Acting as spokeswomen for the event, their generous donation, profits from "Mama/Who Do You Think You Are," was the largest individual contribution.

During the second week of March, 141 stories about the Girls appeared in British newspapers. In Parliament, the Chancellor of the Exchequer (treasury) quoted them: "I'll tell you what I want, what I really want . . . rising living standards for the next five years." Prime Minister Tony Blair claimed "Wannabe" was one of the records he would most want if stranded on a deserted island. Some of the publicity was not exactly the kind the Girls wanted, however. Since the release of "Wannabe," 13 former boyfriends had sold stories to British tabloids, and according to the Girls, many details were completely fabricated.

Later in March, the Girls scored another triumph. At the Capital FM Awards, they were named London's Favorite Female Group. At the same time, *Spice Girls: Girl Power!*, full of colorful pictures, information, and quotations, went on sale at London's Virgin Megastore. The Girls signed autographs for the crowd. "We're doing it, girls, so can you," Emma wrote in the book. On March 30, the Girls launched Channel 5, a new TV network, and in April, they flew to New York City to appear on *Saturday Night Live*.

Invited to appear on Saturday Night Live, *the Girls strut their stuff at a dress rehearsal. Their own star status did not prevent them from being thrilled when they met the respected actor Robert De Niro backstage.*

Following the release of *Spice: The Official Video, Volume One*, the Girls signed a lucrative deal with Pepsico, which launched a major summer promotion. The Girls would also benefit from a worldwide summer TV commercial blitz featuring the song "Move Over" from their upcoming album. The Girls were ecstatic. They could not hope for better publicity.

In May, the Girls flew to the Cannes Film Festival in southern France, a yearly event that draws the international film set. Appearing in a blaze of flashbulbs on the steps of the prestigious Palais Cinema, they literally stopped traffic. In full Spice regalia, the Girls swept into a press conference, seated themselves like royalty on the podium, and quickly began putting everyone in their place. "Now whoever's got the biggest smile and the nicest vibes," began Geri calmly. "This man at the front has got really bad body language," interrupted Mel B. The room exploded in laughter.

The more opportunities the Spice Girls have to express their Girl Power message, the better. But, exactly what is Girl Power? Each has her own idea. For Mel C it means a girl can play soccer too. For Emma it is an equal relationship between men and women. Geri believes it is making the most of what you have. Even if you are short—think tall. Mel B's Girl Power is appreciating her mixed-race roots. For Victoria, it means finding your true self and some real friends.

The Spice Girls shared a dream when they first met in July 1994. Through hard work and sheer determination, they took their collective dream much further than any of them had imagined possible. The Girls had not just started a singing group. They had started a movement, and in the summer of 1997, things would get even spicier.

6

SPICE WORLD

In May 1997, the Girls flew to New York City for a blitz of talk-show appearances. They chatted with Regis Philbin and Kathie Lee Gifford on their morning show, dubbing Kathy Lee an honorary Spice Girl. On Rosie O'Donnell's show, the Girls offered Rosie the choice of the honorary title "Tough" or "Sassy." Good-natured Rosie thought she would like to be both.

Returning to England, the Girls' songwriting talents were recognized when they won the Ivor Novello Awards for International Hit of the Year and Best Selling British Single. A week later, they began filming *Spice World*, a celebration of their meteoric success. Set in ultrahip '90s' London, the movie is a boisterous, satirical adventure that chronicles a busy week of performances, rehearsals, recording sessions, press conferences, and photo shoots leading up to their first live concert. The film's cast includes Roger Moore, the group Meatloaf, and cameo appearances by Elton John and Elvis Costello.

Highlights of the film's wild romp through a hectic week include a comic flashforward with the Girls dressed as mothers, the Girls being lead on an army-style obstacle

---

Dressed alike in snappy white outfits, the Girls appear on Hollywood Boulevard in Los Angeles atop a double-decker bus for the U.S. premiere of their film Spice World.

course by an eccentric dance captain, and a hilarious encounter with adoring aliens. Through it all, the five manage to defend their Girl Power credo and stay true to themselves.

The Girls worked on the script, and they all played themselves, but with a little exaggeration. In a comic parody of her "Posh" persona, all of Victoria's lines are about fashion. Baby Emma uses her sweet smile to get the group out of jams. Geri is always talking about something she has read. Practical Mel C worries about the fans if the concert is canceled, while tigress Mel B shows plenty of "big attitude." In *Spice World: The Official Book of the Movie*, which documents the Girls' behind-the-scenes experiences, Victoria wrote: "The day we filmed our concert at Albert Hall was the best day on the film for all of us." Emma agreed: "The whole crowd was dancing and had all the moves, and they were singing along!"

For two months, the Girls, all notoriously late risers (except Mel C), had to be in costume and makeup at 6 A.M. Sometimes filming continued until 8 P.M., and they still had to fit interviews, photo sessions, even the filming of a TV commercial for Walkers Crisps (a leading British potato-chip company) into their hectic days. Still, the fun-loving Spices had more than a few laughs with the cast and crew, often improvising hilarious new lines during a take. "Sometimes we'd just crack up and wouldn't be able to do a take again because we'd be silly," wrote Emma.

During the filming, many of the songs on *Spice World*, the Girls' second album, were written in a mobile recording studio on the set. "We were having a laugh and running around doing different scenes. So the vibe was always good when we went into the recording caravan at night to write songs," Emma wrote. Once filming ended at the beginning of August, the Girls had three weeks to lay down final tracks for the album. Again they worked with the same production teams who had helped to make *Spice* such a success. The zesty "Spice Up Your Life" is Mel C's favorite song. "We always wanted to do a carnival tune and write a song for the world after all our traveling," she wrote. All the songs on *Spice World* reflect an international sensibility. The album is a heart-felt expression of the Girls' heightened under-standing of love and friendship after a year in the spotlight. On *Spice World*, as on *Spice*, the Girls harmonize and freestyle off each other, trading lyrics and background vocals in a non-stop whirl of driving energy. The catchy hip-hop, salsa, and R&B mix of danceable tunes are all easy to sing along to, making the album another surefire hit.

In an explosion of marketing, Spice Girls merchandise appeared everywhere. In London, a little girl happily clutches her Spice Girls dolls, one of the many spin-offs that have made the real Girls very wealthy.

With the tracks for *Spice World* delivered to Virgin and their movie in the editing room, in September 1997 the Girls were busy signing endorsement deals, including one with PMS, one of the world's top manufacturers, to create Spice Girls merchandise. They filmed an ad for a Polaroid Spicecam. Faberge would create a scented *Spice Up Your Life* CD single to promote the launch of a new fragrance, Impulse Spice. The chocolate company Cadbury would pro-duce five chocolate Spice Girl figurines. There was also a lucrative deal to sell Spice-theme products in supermarkets. The Girls now ranked number 32 in *Forbes* magazine's annu-al list of the world's highest-paid entertainers.

With Spice fever raging, imitators like the Spicey Girls and the Spiced Girls began turning up at industry parties and award shows. Look-alikes Nice 'n' Spicey crashed the BRIT Awards in February, fooling even Emma's mother, who shouted "Emma!" as the clones swept past.

The fall of 1997 was a time of whirlwind tours. In Turkey, the Girls appeared in a blaze of smoke and flashing lights before 11,000 screaming fans at Istanbul's Abdi Ipeki stadium. Bouncing around on a giant roller-coaster set with glitter-sprayed minicars poised at each peak, the five performed a concert of songs from their two albums before closing the show with a high-powered "Wannabe." Proclaimed the London *Sun*, "Fab Five Turk 'Em by Storm."

Continuing their appearances, the Girls previewed *Spice Up Your Life* at a press party in Granada, Spain, and flew to India for the star-studded Channel V Music Awards. They sang two songs and presented an award to a female Indian performer. Back again in England, the Girls announced that "Mama" would be among songs by the world's top artists on the commemorative album *Diana, Princess of Wales Tribute*. They also appealed to fans to honor British war heroes at London's Royal British Legion Poppy Appeal (English Veterans Day). Wearing black, the Girls took turns reading stanzas from Laurence Binyon's war poem "For the Fallen."

At the beginning of November, the Girls appeared in the Netherlands for the Dutch MTV Awards. After the show, a volcano that had been rumbling in the Spice camp erupted. The Girls fired their manager, Simon Fuller. From now on, they would make their own business decisions.

The girls next stop was Rome, where they were promoting *Spice World.* When hundreds of fans mobbed the street outside their hotel, the Girls appeared on the balcony, threw flowers to the crowd, and sang "Spice Up Your Life" and "Too Much." Returning to England to rehearse for a November 29th TV special, *An Audience with the Spice Girls*, the five went on BBC Radio to dispel rumors that Simon Fuller's dismissal boded a breakup, insisting "We are stronger than ever." They certainly seemed to be. After singing at the annual Royal Variety Performance, the Girls had the honor of meeting Queen Elizabeth. *Smash Hits'* readers named them Best British Group for the second year in a row. *Spice World* was garnering positive reviews and selling 103,000 copies a week

Wearing the traditional Indian women's dress, the sari, Mel C, Geri, and Victoria perform in New Delhi at the Channel V Music Awards. The Girls, who were the main attraction, walked off with two awards.

in the United States. *People* raved, "Thanks to savvy production and a cheeky sense of fun, the Spice Girls have already outlived their predicted shelf-life."

In mid-November, the Girls' next book, *Real Life: Real Spice: The Official Story,* was released in book stores. In it, the five offered advice to their readers, such as this tip from Geri: "Walk away from negativity. As long as you are a good person and have integrity, you will always get what you deserve." A few weeks later, the UPN channel presented the first U.S. TV network Spice Girls special—*Spice Girls: Too Much Is Never Enough.* The show featured high-spirited interviews, behind-the-scenes recording sessions, and a sneak peak at their film *Spice World.*

As 1997 ended and a new year began, the Girls kept up their hectic schedule. In New York City, they made the rounds of talk shows and, at a press conference were asked if they considered themselves good teenage role models. Mel C responded: "We're quite normal and we've made the most of ourselves. We're not six-feet-tall models with eating disorders."

From New York it was on to Los Angeles, where the movie *Spice World* premiered at Mann's Chinese Theatre. The Girls scored a huge hit as they stepped out of their limo onto a red carpet and into a cheering, celebrity-studded crowd. At a Planet Hollywood party, their handprints, footprints, and signatures were immortalized in cement. *Spice World* hit theaters the next day, earning $11.3 million in its first week. Although reviews were mixed, kids, with parents in tow, flocked in droves to see it. With a boost from the film, the album *Spice World,* which had already sold 10 million copies worldwide, jumped to number three on the *Billboard* charts.

At the end of January, while rehearsing in Ireland for a European tour, they triumphed again when the American Music Awards honored them with Best Group, Best Album, and Best New Artist awards. After three weeks of intensive rehearsals, the Girls kicked off their tour with a performance in Dublin, where crowds of adoring teenage girls screamed and wept at the sight of their beloved idols.

On the tour, which included appearances in Paris, Vienna, and Scandinavia, the Girls performed with a futuristic stainless-steel set, a dazzling light show, and five male backup dancers. Included in the frenetic concerts were six costume changes, roller-skating, acrobatics, ballet, and dances from around the world. In a spectacular finale, the Spice Girls boarded the "Spiceship" and were transported via a huge video screen to "Spice World."

Despite the success of their tour, all was not well in Spice World. On May 27, 1998, when the five were supposed to appear on the BBC's National Lottery draw, Geri was nowhere to be seen. The Girls' publicist said Geri was suffering from stomach pain. The press, however, reported that after leaving Helsinki, Finland, earlier that day, the five had argued all the way back to England on their private jet. When, a day later, the Girls flew to Oslo, Norway, for the final leg of their tour, Geri was not with them. Remarkably, the four restaged the dances and vocal routines in just two hours and presented a brilliant, flawless show to thousands of cheering fans.

On May 31 Geri stunned fans around the world when she released a statement confirming that she had left the group because of "differences between us." From Elton John's villa in southern France, the remaining Girls issued a follow-up statement: "We are upset and saddened by Geri's departure but we are very supportive in whatever she wants to do." They reassured fans, "The Spice Girls are here to stay."

Although the five had become four, British viewers got one last look at the Girls as a quintet when a prerecorded performance of the song "Viva Forever" was shown on the show *Top of the Pops.* Shaken by Geri's departure, the Girls nevertheless continued their hectic schedule in the following weeks. Mel C flew to Dublin to record vocals for the group's third album, which was to feature solo performances. A few days later in Modena, Italy, the four Spices harmonized on "Viva Forever" with famous opera tenor Luciano Pavarotti as the fifth Spice, when they performed at the War Child Concert, a benefit to raise funds for a children's village in Liberia, Africa.

In the middle of June, the Girls kicked off their U.S. tour in Miami, Florida. On the same day, *Spice World* was released in stores. It would soon top the *Billboard* charts as the best-selling U.S. video.

In their Palm Beach hotel, a revved-up Mel B told the BBC's Kevin Greening, "We're very excited and we can't wait to get up there and show all the Americans what we're made of." Two weeks after the break with Geri, the four Spices were adapting well to life as a quartet. They understood that it was time for her to move on to other projects.

After 25 shows, the four Spices were in high gear. In the explosive 18–number spectacle, rousing renditions of "Sisters Are Doin' It for

Themselves" and "We Are a Family" brought thousands of American girls leaping to their feet. Miami was a success—even without Geri. Mel B soon announced plans to record a solo album and a duet with American singer Missy Elliot for a movie sound track. The other Spices were also planning solo projects. Asked if the solo records meant the band would split up, Mel B replied, "We're friends, not a band. So we can't split up, can we?"

In June, Geri was being considered for parts in a remake of the TV show *Charlie's Angels* and a British kids TV show, along with roles in Hollywood movies. At New York City's Madison Square Garden show on July 1, which had sold out in a record-breaking 12 minutes—Victoria told *Entertainment Weekly*, "We wish her all the

In their first live performance since Geri had left the group, the remaining Girls perform at a benefit concert with tenor Luciano Pavarotti, who temporarily became the fifth Spice.

luck in the world. . . . The most important thing is our friendship."

As of July 1998, *Spice World*, the movie, had grossed $77 million worldwide, and combined sales of the two albums had reached a whopping $30 million. "Viva Forever," released in July in Britain, climbed to number one, making the Spice Girls the only group ever to have seven number-one hits. In August, the Girls negotiated with Elizabeth Arden for a Spice perfume and with Pepsico for a new promotion featuring a four-track, live-concert CD. In September, they wrapped up their world tour with two concerts in Sheffield, England. The Girls, who plan to be godmothers to one another's children, are now managing themselves. Victoria arranges merchandising; Mel C is the record-company liaison; Emma oversees personnel and charity; and Mel B handles touring. Their third album is planned for late 1998.

Whether the four remaining Spices continue as a quartet, branching out to do solo projects, or eventually go their own ways, the mark the Spice Girls have made in the history of pop music can never be erased. Having breathed new life into pop and spiced it up with a distinctly Girl-Powered flavor, they inspired an entire generation of the world's young people to be true to themselves and their dreams, but to have fun doing it. The Spice Girls were five unknown English girls, five "wannabes," who forged an honest and caring friendship, worked hard, and through the force of their indomitable spirits launched a Spicy movement. The world will never be the same again. "When you're feeling sad and low/We will take you where you want to go/Laughing, dancing, everything is free/All you need is positivity."

CHRONOLOGY

1972   Geraldine Estelle Halliwell is born on August 6.

1974   Melanie Jayne Chisholm is born on January 12 in Liverpool; Victoria Addams is born on April 7.

1975   Melanie Janine Brown is born on May 29 in Leeds.

1976   Emma Lee Bunton is born on January 21 in Finchley, North London.

1994   Five-girl group forms and begins living and training together; chooses name "Spice" for band.

1995   Sign on with Virgin Records and manager Simon Fuller.

1996   Release debut single "Wannabe" in Britain, tops the charts; release *Spice* album; win *Smash Hits* Awards for Best British Act, Best New Act, and Best Video; host *Top of the Pops* TV show on Christmas Day; turn on London's Christmas Lights; "Say You'll Be There" is released, shoots to number one in U.K; "Wannabe" hits number one in 31 countries; "2Become1" is released, hits number one in U.K.; *Spice* is best selling album of the year in U.K.

1997   *Spice* album is released in United States; first issue of *Spice*, the official Spice Girl magazine is released; Virgin launches official Spice Girl website; win Best Video and Best Single at BRIT Awards; record second album *Spice World;* perform at the Prince of Wales's Trust Concert; stage first large venue concert in Turkey; perform charity benefit in South Africa, meet Prince Charles, Prince Harry, and President Nelson Mandela; "Mama/Who Do You Think You Are" is released in Britain and hits number one; named London's Favourite Female Group at Capital FM Awards; film the movie *Spice World;* "Say You'll Be There" is released in United States; win Ivor Novello Awards for International Hit of the Year and Best Selling British Single; "Spice Up Your Life" is released in Britain, hits number one; launch Channel 5, a new TV network in U.K.; sign a deal with Pepsico; sign endorsement deals with manufacturers for Spice Girls product lines; meet Queen Elizabeth; dismiss manager Simon Fuller.

1998   Premier of *Spice World* in the United States; win American Music Awards as Best Group, Best Album, and Best New Artist; "Too Much" hits number one in U.K.; "Viva Forever" hits number one, makes Spice Girls first group ever to have seven number one hit singles in Britain; begin a world tour in Europe; Geri leaves the group; begin U.S. tour without Geri; plan to continue as quartet with possible solo performances.

ACCOMPLISHMENTS

Singles/Albums

1996 "Wannabe" (single)
"Say You'll Be There" (single)
"2Become1" (single)
Spice (album)

1997 "Mama/Who Do You Think You Are" (single)
"Spice Up Your Life" (single)
Spice World (album)

1998 "Too Much" (single)
"Viva Forever" (single)

Videos/Films/TV/Performance

1996 *Say You'll Be There* (video)
Top of the Pops (TV show appearance)

1997 *Spice Girls: Too Much Is Never Enough* (TV special)
An Audience with the Spice Girls (TV special)
Spice Girls, Girl Power! Live in Istanbul (video)
Girls Talk! (video)
Spice Girls: One Hour of Girl Power! (video)
Girl Power: The Unauthorized Biography of the Spice Girls (video)
Spice: The Official Video, Volume One (video)
Prince of Wales's Trust Concert (concert)
Istanbul, Turkey Performance (concert)
South African Benefit Performance (concert)

1998 *Spice World: The Spice Girls Movie* (movie)
World Tour (concerts)
U.S. Tour (concerts)

Awards

1996 *Smash Hits* Awards: Best British Act, Best New Act, Best Video.

1997 BRIT Awards: Best Video, Best Single; Capital FM Award: London's Favourite Female Group; Ivor Novello Awards: International Hit of the Year, Best Selling British Single; MTV Video Music Award: Best Dance Video; Irish Music Award: Best International Act; *Billboard* Music Awards: New Artist of the Year, Album of the Year.

1998 American Music Awards: Best Group, Best Album, Best New Artist.

FURTHER READING

Dimery, Robert, editor. *Live Spice!* London: Omnibus Books, 1998.

Golden, Anna Louise. *The Spice Girls.* New York: Ballantine Books, 1997.

Joseph, Michael, and David Richter, Ski Newton. *Spice Universe.* London: Arrowhead Books, 1998.

The Spice Girls. *Real Life, Real Spice: The Official Story.* London: Zone/Chameleon Books, 1997.

The Spice Girls. *Spice Girls: Girl Power!* Secaucus, NJ: Carol Publishing Group, Citadel Press Book, 1997.

The Spice Girls. *Spice World: The Official Book of the Movie.* New York: Crown Publishers, Three Rivers Press, 1997.

Spice Girls: The Hottest Band Around. London: Virgin Books, 1996.

Offical Spice Girls Website
http://channel3.vmg.co.uk/spicegirls

Fan Club
Girl Power! P.O. Box 8863, Red Bank, N.J. 07701

ABOUT THE AUTHOR

Nancy Shore is a freelance writer and editor living in New York City. Her book, *Amelia Earhart*, was published by Chelsea House in 1987.

INDEX